George Henry Loskiel, J. Max Hark

Extempore on a Wagon

A metrical Narrative of a Journey from Bethlehem, Pa., to the Indian town

of Goshen, Ohio, in the autumn of 1803

George Henry Loskiel, J. Max Hark

Extempore on a Wagon
A metrical Narrative of a Journey from Bethlehem, Pa., to the Indian town of
Goshen, Ohio, in the autumn of 1803

ISBN/EAN: 9783337062941

Printed in Europe, USA, Canada, Australia, Japan

Cover: Foto ©ninafisch / pixelio.de

More available books at **www.hansebooks.com**

Extempore on a Wagon;

—A—

Metrical Narrative

OF A

JOURNEY FROM BETHLEHEM, PA., TO THE INDIAN
TOWN OF GOSHEN, OHIO, IN THE
AUTUMN OF 1803,

BY

George Henry Loskiel,

EPISCOPUS FRATRUM.

TRANSLATED WITH NOTES
BY
J. Max Hark.

LANCASTER, PA.
PUBLISHED BY SAMUEL H. ZAHM & Co.
1887.

INTRODUCTION.

SEVERAL years ago Mr. Samuel H. Zahm found, hidden away among a mass of old papers, a time-stained little manuscript, carefully stitched together, and bearing the peculiar title: *Extempore auf dem Wagen—Br. Loskiel.* It was written in a feminine hand, in clear, even beautiful German script. The discoverer's curiosity being excited, he instituted a careful research, and traced the manuscript back to his great-grandfather M. Zahm, but could find no positive evidence as to how it came into his ancestor's possession. It is not unlikely, however, that it came into the Zahm family, then members of the Moravian Church, directly through Sister Anna Rosa (or Rosina) Kliest, the original writer and owner of the manuscript, and one of the three persons whose journey it describes.

Sr. Kliest seems to have been Bishop Loskiel's diarist and a kind of private secretary on this journey; and the hand-writing of the manuscript has been identified as her own. She probably copied it at, or soon after, the time of its composition, from the original autograph manuscript of the author, which is now in the possession of Prof. Abraham Beck, of Lititz, Pa. A comparison of the two manuscripts shows them to be of apparently the same age, and Sr. Kliest's to be an exact, verbatim copy of the original; the only difference being that the copy is divided into stanzas, which is not the case with Loskiel's original. In the translation, which has been made from the former, this form has also been followed. In every other respect, too, the translator has scrupulously followed the manuscript, aiming first and last at literalness, and faithfulness in reproducing, as far as at all possible, the exact rhyme, and metre, without any attempt to correct its faults, to convert its doggerel into poetry, or to make any change or improvements in the sentiments or form of the original.

The author of the curious and not unskillful *Extempore on a Wagon*, George Henry Loskiel, was the son of a Lutheran minister at Angermunde, in Curland, where he was born on Nov. 7, 1740. When a young man he went to Barby, in Prussia, and there joined the Moravian Church on Dec. 26, 1759, and betook himself diligently to the study of medicine and theology. In 1765 he went as teacher to the Moravian Paedagogium, at Niesky, but already the next year removed to Neuwied; two years after to Marienborn, and in 1769 to Amsterdam. On June 27, 1771, he married *Maria Magdalena Barlach*. Distinguished for his piety no less than his ability as a preacher and a practical manager, he was appointed to the responsible office, in 1782, of Superintendent of the Mission in Livonia, and at the same time agent for the Moravian Church in Russia. It was about this time that Br. Loskiel wrote his well-known and in many respects excellent "History of the Mission of the United Brethren Among the Indians of North America." This remained his chief literary work; though he was also the author of other works, and a hymn writer of no mean ability, as the hymns from his pen still in use in the Moravian hymnal bear witness.

In 1801, while at Herrnhut, Br. Loskiel received a call to Bethlehem, Pa., as President of the Board having the oversight of the Moravian Church with its missions in America. He arrived there on July 23, 1802, having, however, first been solemnly consecrated to the episcopate, on March 14, 1802 just before his departure from Herrnhut. It was in his official capacity, as Bishop and President of the Board, that he, accompanied by his wife and Sr. Anna Rosa Kliest, undertook the journey to Goshen, in Tuscarawas county, Ohio, so graphically described in the following pages. Its object was to hold a conference of missionaries at the latter place, for the full discussion of the whole work of Indian Missions in the West. The Bishop left Bethlehem on Sept. 12, 1803, and arrived at Goshen a few days before the opening of the conference, which was in session from October 10th to 21st, on which latter date Bishop Loskiel solemnly ordained the young Br. John Ben Haven to the ministry. This being the first ordination service ever witnessed by the Indians, made a deep and wholesome impression upon them.

The return trip to Bethlehem was begun on October 29, and in due time the good Bishop was again in the midst of his beloved brethren on the Lehigh. In 1812 he received an appointment to the Directory at Herrnhut, but failing health, and the war with Great Britain, made it impossible for him to leave the country. Two years after, on February 23, 1814, he peacefully closed his earthly pilgrimage, and entered upon his heavenly rest. He was buried in the old Moravian graveyard at Bethlehem, where so many of the devoted and saintly ministers of that venerable Church are sleeping, side by side with as many of the "brown hearts" and black, for whom they labored, and with whom they shall rise again when the Lord comes to make up his jewels.

So far as known the two manuscripts of *Extempore on a Wagon* above described are the only copies in existence. Certainly the following pages contain the only translation ever made of the quaint old narrative.

J. M. H.

LANCASTER, Pa., May, 1887.

EXTEMPORE ON A WAGON.

By Brother Loskiel.
Sept. 12, 1803.

At length there dawned the happy day,
The glorious one, we well may say,
Whereon we three [1] our tour began
To visit the much feared Red Man.

Long is the journey we've begun,
Nor is there many an harder one ;
The mountains are immensely high,
E'en higher than most birds can fly ;

The roads so miserably poor,
That we had rather made the tour
On foot, but that we knew its length
Would overtax our feeble strength.

---

[1] Bishop Loskiel, his wife, and Anna Rosa Kliest.

For what with rocks, and stumps and trees,
Despair doth oft the traveler seize ;
And rivers, creeks, and swampy ground
Have oft the boldest courage drowned.

All this to us doth hard appear :
And yet e'en were it far more drear,
We still should gladly forward go,
Since Christ our Lord ordained it so.

Therefore I'll straight begin to tell
What us and our team befell,
How we and our horses fared,
Thankful to Him who hath us spared.

At Bethlehem,[2] the mother town,
Who hath already daughters grown,
We left behind us small and great,
Content with their allotted state.

We took their fervent love along
To stay with us all scenes among :
To comfort us each step we take,
Their hearts and ours as one to make.

---

[2] The seat of government of the Moravian Church in America ; founded in 1741, on the Lehigh river, in Northampton county, Pa.

Extempore on a Wagon.

One travels lightly with such love
That lifts the soul to things above ;
And Jesus' blood so filled us three,
We could not aught but happy be.

With Sister Schaaf we went as far
As Emmaus, where friend Molthers are,
Whose daughter I as Baptist straight
Unto the Lord must dedicate.

I gladly served, in thankful mood,
While we all three as sponsors stood,
As Annie Schaaf and Horsefield, too ;
Who held the babe? This Rose must do.

Then forward ; by friend Molther's side,
Who on his horse along doth ride
As friendship's guard, till Trexler's place,
Where grateful sleep not long delays.

Then we go on from place to place,
As we three travel on apace,
Until dear Lititz comes in sight,
Where we must halt at least o'er night.

For Brother Rixeker[3] lives here,
And Brother Jungman too is near,
The Lord these two us given hath
As guides along the perilous path.

And, by the way, 'twas good to rest
Trusting the Saviour's each behest,
Rejoicing in the brethren's love
Which us most sensibly did move.

When we depart no sound is heard,
Not e'en our driver speaks a word ;
In silence we a farewell wave,
To all the loved ones sleeping safe.

The road us soon through Manheim took,
Which doth like one long furrow look !
The inn we reach, 'tis named " The Goose ;"
The landlord " Hans," we may suppose.

---

[3] Jacob Rixeker, or Ricksecker, born in Donegal April 13,
1746, was a farmer and in June 1799 had driven the first team
with goods from Bethlehem to the settlement at Gnadenhutten,
Ohio. Peter Jungman, a son of the missionary, John George
Jungman, at the time living in retirement at Bethlehem (?). Both
Ricksecker and Jungman were members of the congregation at
Lititz.

Mountjoy's our halting place to-night,
Where our dear Peters, with delight,
A resting place for us prepare,
And for our horses' comfort care.

The roads now grow amazing bad,
Such rattling, rumbling, ne'er we had,
The bumps, to right and left, declare,
Both loud and plain, how bad they were.

Now suddenly there is a thud ;
Rose Anna fell into the mud !
And lost thereby one of her shoes,
In finding which some time we lose.

Swatara was the first large stream
O'er which we crossed,—and it did seem
The Daily Word [2] expressed our thought :
Our Strength and Refuge is our God.

———

[1] Since 1731 the Moravian Church has issued an annual collection of "Daily Words and Doctrinal Texts," containing an Old and a New Testament text for each day of the year, the former chosen by lot. These texts were accepted by all as divinely given watchwords, for each one's guidance, comfort, and direction in the work and life of each day.

To Middletown we onward went,
Where with kind friends the night we spent,
Then early from our sleep awake,
And for the Susquehanna make.

This wide stream here we shallow found,
And soon have crossed it safe and sound,
Proceeding slowly on our way,
To where we can for dinner stay.

The hostess, rather grum was she,
And not as friendly looked as we ;
All we could do was quite in vain
Nor served a kindly look to gain.

Her big dog Phylax by her stood,
But seemed to be in friendlier mood,
And thanked us for the gifts we gave,
In language such as canines have.

To Carlisle we by evening come,
Where we are made to feel at home,
Although the rats we have to fight
Destroy for us the peace of night.

Extempore on a Wagon.

We early have to turn our face
Away from this most friendly place.
Noon brings us to another friend,
Where we the midday hour spend.

To-day I walked the greater part,
Up hill and down,—nor found it hard ;
For in the peace of Christ I went,
Who me His constant presence lent.

But all at once two horsemen came
And stopped us, calling me by name.
How I to them thus known could be
A question is that puzzles me.

At Westmoreland they both reside,
Where wife and children now abide.
And they were going whence we came,
We three whose home is Bethlehem.

That we no letters had to send
Full twenty times we did lament ;
We thousand greetings send for all
At Bethlehem and Nazareth Hall.

At Shippensburg both drink and food,
Praise be to God! were very good;
And just as good our place of rest,
Our sleep was of the very best!

Of Blickensderfers two appear,
And Tschudy, come from Lititz here;
We all rejoice most heartily,
And greet each other lovingly.

They early riding on ahead,
We follow, after farewells said.
May God those people well repay
For all their kindness through our stay!

At Strasburg where at noon we stop,
We looked up at the mountain top
That 'fore us rose so steep and high;
No use of hurry here, thought I!

Here too, however, soon we find
The people very dear and kind.
They strengthen us with bounteous cheer,
For our day's work doth hard appear.

We now ascend the first steep hill ;
With sorrow it my muse did fill !
It made us more than once lament ;
Yet Jesus ever with us went.

We felt His presence palpably,
Oft so that we could almost see
His helpful arm and blessed face ;
Which filled our hearts with strengthening grace.

More arduous was the second hill,
'Twas steeper far, and rockier still ;
This too, howe'er, we crossed to-day,
With weary limbs, but hearts still gay.

I climbed the hills in cheerful mood,
Armed with a slender staff of wood :
And my dear little company
In the same manner followed me.

The weather's not at all amiss,
To God be all the praise for this !
The sky was cloudy, but the rain
Held back till we could ride again.

But when the wagon I once more
Had reached, it straight began to pour !
And now we gave our thanks anew
To the dear Lord so good and true.

Now Emmetsburg we soon can view,
Both wearied and perspired through.
Though rest and nourishment we find,
The *feeling* seems to us not kind.

We therefore early leave this place,
And straightway hasten on apace
To cross the third hill, rough but grand,
That doth majestic 'fore us stand.

It is the highest of the three,
And also may the steepest be ;
Yet I climbed up and down its sides
With strength such as the Lord provides.

My Mary's and Rose Anna's mood
For climbing, too, seemed pretty good ;
But soon, although they did their best,
'Twas plain they felt the need of rest.

Extempore on a Wagon.

The weather was for walking fine :
Cooled by the rain, the bright sunshine
Now made the air so pure and clear,
Our morning hymn was sweet to hear.

Thus all in bright and happy mood,
And filled with fervent gratitude,
God helped us on our pilgrimage
O'er what had been its roughest stage.

To Jamisons' our steps we bent :
I'd felt a strong presentiment
From far, that here sweet rest we'd find
Alike for body and for mind.

And so it was.   These people kind
In serving us true pleasure find.
The house is filled with God's own peace,
And gladly here we rest at ease.

I take a walk, as well content
As though I 'long the Lehigh went !
Communion with the Man of Woes
It is that such sweet peace bestows.

Dear Sister Loskiel stayed behind,
After our toil some rest to find,
Though not in sinful idleness ;
While Rose's pen seemed tireless.

Good Brother Jacob's heart was light
Because we were so far all right ;
And Brother Peter, all alone,
Wrote busily,—what, is not known.

After our much enjoyed rest,
We start again towards the west,
Where, fourteen miles away, we see
A fourth hill that must crossed be.

Yet one more loving look we give
To where the Jamisons do live.
We count their children—nine in all ;
God bless each one, both great and small !

As onward now our way we wend,
The hills seem ne'er to take an end,
And many looked quite like to them
We knew so well at Bethlehem.

A wilderness of rocks is here,
Both high and rugged, dark and drear ;
Wherever we our eyes may set,
By nothing but gray rocks they're met.

'Tis Sideling Mountain ; but the name
Of Mount of Patience fits the same ;
For, haste the traveler as he may,
Its summit still seems far away.

The weather being warm and close,
In streams the perspiration flows
The whole day long, from every pore,
And leaves us weary and foot-sore.

Nor does our halting place bring rest ;
At Wylie's 'tis,—a vile rats' nest !
So journeying on, lit by the moon,
At Martin's we arrive full soon.

The landlady at first was grum,
She wished us home, and scolded some—
When all at once she changed her song ;
Worn out from scolding us so long !

Quite friendly she became and kind ;
Our comfort sought with eager mind ;
At last came penitent to crave
Our pardon, which we gladly gave.

Next morning, without harm or loss,
The Juniata soon we cross.
No house nor bird doth meet the eye ;
It is a pilgrimage most dry !

But yet we all were happy still,
Accepting all as God's own will.
Our joy in Him was our might ;
To praise Him was our souls' delight.

As every morning, so to-day,
Re-echoed far our morning lay,
From happy hearts a grateful song,
Resounding all the hills along.

To travel is a weariness
When one no faster can progress,
And oft no further goes each day
Than from Herrnhut to Kleinwelke.[5]

---

[5] Two Moravian settlements in Saxony, 16 to 20 miles apart.

We come to Bedford, but can stay
Scarcely a quarter of a day.
Here Rose a former pupil finds,
And visits her, quite to our minds.

We early start, after our rest,
To reach grim Alleghany's crest,
A mount so bulky and so tall
'Twould make the Hengstberg look quite small !

Our dinner and our night's bivouac
We make here on this giant's back ;
The road was good, the weather clear,
But birds here very scarce appear,

Although with pleasure once I heard
The drumming of a pheasant bird ;
And joyfully, in grateful mood,
We felt that God made all things good.

To-day we not a little hear
Of thieves and robbers being near ;
But know God is our Rock and Tower,
He holds e'en robbers in His power.

Our night's halt at the "Indian King"
To none of us much sleep did bring;
For rats were there in such a herd
The wagon I as couch preferred.

Our beds here nearer heaven lay
Than last night's; but I grieve to say
We several miles must travel on
Before the mountain's top we've won.

Next morning wearily we ride
Still up the Alleghany's side;
Till we at length the cabin see,
Which on its summit's said to be.

But the descent was harder still!
Who in the wagon stayed fared ill;
While who, like I, on foot did go,
Escaped full many a bitter woe!

The Alleghanies seem to me
Much like the Giant Hills to be,
Whose heads into the clouds do reach,
And yet high timber grows on each.

With mine host Sewitz, where we dined,
Our meal was scant, the same in kind
As almost daily was our lot :
'Twas sausage, tongue and ham we got.

We next must pass through Somerset ;
I fain would stop in this hamlet,
But the majority say no,
So I must yield, and further go.

At Kilian Grey's we spend the night,
As comfortably as we might,
Where swarming rats on the rampage
In constant battle us engage.

Next morning Laurel Hill we cross ;
To picture it I'm at a loss.
The highest point 'tis said to be,
The worst it is undoubtedly !

I mounted it right cheerfully,
And praised God's power heartily.
Such works his wondrous might display,
Preserving them from day to day.

The prospect from the summit here
Was beautiful, immense, and clear ;
A pity, though, it makes one feel
America's unfinished still !

More difficult the ascent grows ;   ₁
For our poor feet 'tis full of woes,
A very cross ! They seem to say,
" We are too old to toil this way !"

For six long hours we traveled on,
Then rest two hours—'twas hardly won !—
At Jones's, where our beasts and we
Much longer could contented be.

At Hartman's we the night might spend,
But rather our footsteps bend
Towards Byerly's, where, though 'tis cold,
Sweet sleep doth soon us all enfold.

A child that just had "walloped"[6] been,
Screamed lustily, as all, I ween,
Are wont to do when smart the blows
The parent's rod on them bestows.

---

[6] "Geledert " was the mother's expression.

Extempore on a Wagon.

Three Chestnut ridges yet remain
For us to cross, 'twill cause some pain ;
Though not as steep and long they are
As some which we have crossed thus far.

We with one Mueller did intend
To take our dinner,—but no friend
Was he of hospitality.
To have us go he liked to see !

At Philip Null's as halting place
We rested for a little space—
Not long ; for soon our steps we bend
To where we hope the night to spend.

But there we disappointment reap :
Waldhauer no more inn doth keep !
Yet hospitably he's inclined,
And gives us beds—after a kind !

The sisters with contented mind
Their's in the spring-house needs must find ;
While in the wagon I must camp,
But find it hard and cold and damp.

Next morning Pittsburg is our aim ;
But ere at eve we reach the same,
Much bumping up and down the hills
Makes it a day of many ills.

We there expect some stay to make,
And sorely needed rest to take,
And then with strength and courage new
Our pilgrimage again pursue.

We were to meet a person here
At Pittsburg, who did not appear ;
A note from Heckewelder's [7] hand
Makes us the reason understand.

A courier, Brother Fenner's son,
For bringing us the letter won
A fever as his sad reward,
Which made his journey doubly hard.

---

[7] John Heckewelder, born at Bedford, England, on March 12, 1742, scarcely less distinguished than Zeisberger as a devoted Moravian missionary to the Indians, and author of several valuable works relating to the Indians, their language, customs and history. As early as 1762 he, with Fred'k Post, attempted to establish a mission on the Tuscarawas river, in Ohio. At this time he was residing at Gnadenhutten, as agent of the "Society for Propagating the Gospel among the Heathen."

Extempore on a Wagon.

But that the rats the place infest,
Our lot here was the happiest ;
The people anxious seemed to do
For our comfort all they knew.

I walked much, and examined near
The Fortress'[8] beautiful revier,
Within which there is found the source
Whence the Ohio takes its course,

Where the Monongahela's meet
The Alleghany's waters fleet,
And thus the two th' Ohio make—
Their picture I should like to take !

I stood there on the farthest stone,
And gladly did the greatness own
Of our good Lord,—to Him my heart
There a memorial set apart.

At Pittsburg we received and made
Full many visits.   And I laid
The plan to write a little book ;
But all my time our visits took.

---

* Old Fort DuQuesne.

The Feast of Seraphim we hold,
Of which not much is to be told.
In thought we with the angels dwelt,
And thankful for our children felt.

For Nazareth and Bethlehem,
For Hope and Lititz, all of them,
I pray e'en from my inmost heart,
And for our plan in every part.

Amazed I see come up the street
The wagon which was us to meet,
But not till we'd to Georgetown come.
I felt at first like scolding some !

As we had now enjoyed a rest,
We onward straight to Georgetown pressed.
Fording Monongahela's stream—
The weather could not finer seem.

The road to Georgetown from Fort Pitt
Is good enough ; though we find it
No little toil to climb its steeps
As up and down its way it keeps.

And oft its hills are very high,
And steep enough to make one sigh,
For constantly to use the brakes
A traveler's time and patience takes.

Eight miles was what we made to-day,
Then hoped ourselves to rest to lay ;
But found a quilting-frolic there,
Whose racket filled the very air !

At dawn we left the noisy place,
Thankful for our meed of grace ;
And spent from morn to night the day
In toiling o'er our hilly way.

The weather still continued bright ;
Our spirits too were glad and light.
Else there is nought for me to say
As 'twas an uneventful day.

Before a smoke-filled house we sat
And thankful our cold dinner ate ;
Around us stared a wondering crew
Of children. who enjoyed it too.

Our quarters for the night we find
At miller Donkin's, good and kind.
Our hostess claims acquaintance near
With Goshen's pastor, Mortimer.[9]

He writes to her, and she to him,
And she professes high esteem
For ministers, and tells us what
In such is needed, and what not.

Next day we safe to Georgetown came,
Where Beaver is our dear host's name,
Who with his wife treats us so well
That I can scarce in words it tell.

But not for our sakes alone,
As if to honor us, 'twas done ;
But for dear Heckewelder's sake,
As Beaver soon it plain doth make.

---

[9] Benjamin Mortimer, an Englishman by birth, had been Zeisberger's assistant in the mission at Fairfield, Canada, whence
he removed with the mission to organize Goshen, in October,
1798, and serve as pastor of the Indian congregation there. He
died as pastor of the Moravian Church in New York City, on
Nov. 10, 1834.

Extempore on a Wagon.

Hence we in deep humility
Accept the Christian charity,
As though by Heckewelder done,
Who heart and soul of us is one.

We feel indeed here quite at home,
As in and out we go and come ;
We also the occasion take
Some needed purchases to make.

I visit the Ohio oft,
Whose name is to the ear as soft
As it is charming to the eye,
And beauteous, I can testify.

There with my Saviour oft I spake,
Which I a daily practice make ;
For ah ! His love's sweet graciousness
No human tongue can e'er express.

October third again began
Our desert journey ; and it ran
On till the seventh, when in view
Of a new settlement we drew.

How can I e'er the road describe?
'Twould take a far more skillful scribe
Than I ; so I will silent be,
Lest some doubt my veracity.

Enough that 'twas more horrid bad
Than ever I experienced had.
And yet so light our sufferings were
That to complain would not be fair.

For 'twas as good a road, I see,
As *such* a road could ever be !
So we take courage and rejoice
Because the weather was most choice.
　．

I rode a great part of the way,
Upon a steed now white, once gray,
Which, though he'd lost one of his eyes,
I for his safety greatly prize !

Oft too to walk I am content,
In silent, lone enjoyment
Of the blest Trinity's sweet grace,
Which did my sinful heart embrace.

I never felt a moment's fear,
Although of panthers roaming here
No friend, nor anxious wolf or bear
Alone to meet so near their lair.

Here I could vividly conceive
How Christ did in the desert live,
By beasts surrounded night and day,
To thirst and hunger e'er a prey ;

And forty times intensified ;
Besides by Lucifer thrice tried ;
Ah ! hellish pain that must have been
Endured because of our sin !

My heart and eyes brought Him therefore
My warmest thanks, that He thus bore
All that He suffered, willingly,
E'en for a sinful worm like me.

Four nights the trees were our roof,
While angel-guards kept ill aloof ;
And sweetly rang the trees among
Our evening and our morning song.

Before, hard frosts the earth had bound ;
But since for us 'twas needful found
That there should be *no* frost, 'twas done !
We could thank God that there *was* none.

Within our wagon or the tent,
Our thoughts were ever Godward bent.
We sweetly slept.   Wolf, bear, nor snake,
Nor panther e'er kept us awake.

The fifth was our hardest day,
At least so as regards the way ;
Yet gave us to our great delight
Of *Heckewelder's Town* a sight.

For so is Gnadenhutten [10] named,
And Heckewelder widely famed
By strangers in the country round,
'Mongst whom no other name is found.

---

[10] A Moravian settlement on the Tuscarawas river, in Clay
Township, Tuscarawas County, Ohio, founded by Heckewelder
in the spring of 1798, in October of which year Zeisberger and
his Indian colony from Canada also came thither and encamped
around Heckewelder's house preliminary to founding Goshen.
It was on the site of the mission of the same name destroyed
in 1782.

We saw him come down the last hill ;
He recognized us not until
I hailed him. Then what joy was his
And ours ! 'Twas told by many a kiss !

He took us straightway to his town,
Where we, dust-stained and well run down,
So warm a welcome did receive
That no description I can give.

Here then a change our party makes,
Two Brother Huebner [11] with him takes,
And three with Jones and Peters go,
Both glad and welcome to rest so.

But ere the evening's gloom had come,
I view that place of martyrdom,
Where late had flowed the precious blood
Of our brown flock, a crimson flood. [12]

---

[11] Lewis Huebner, pastor of the white settlers on the Tuscarawas reservation since July, 1800, was born at Nazareth, Pa.,
August 8th, 1761, and had ministered to the Moravian Church at
York, and to various other Pennsylvania Congregations, prior
to his removal to Gnadenhutten. He returned to Pennsylvania
in 1804 or 1805.

[12] On March 8, 1782, the mission at Gnadenhutten was ruth-
lessly and totally destroyed by a party of militia under Colonel

That blood so sacred seems to me,
Their memory here should honored be ;
So I at once a plan devise
By which we this might realize.

I had no rest here long to stay,
But soon set out upon the way
To Goshen,[13] where our Indians are,
There gathered 'neath the Gospel's care.

That apostolic man I'd see,
Who cannot too much praised be ;

Williamson, who treacherously and without any provocation imprisoned the congregation of unresisting Moravian Indians, and then deliberately and fiendishly led them forth, two by two, and butchered all but two lads, who made their escape. The Indian Martyrs, for such they were, consisted of 29 men, 27 women, and 34 children, a total of 90 persons. For a full and authentic account of this atrocity see Schweinitz's "Life and Times of David Zeisberger." Ch. XXXV.

[13] Goshen, the objective point of Loskiel's journey, was a settlement of Moravian Indians, founded in October, 1798, by Zeisberger and his colony from Fairfield, Canada. It was situated about seven miles northeast from Gnadenhutten, on the west bank of the Tuscarawas river, in Goshen Township, Tuscarawas County, Ohio. It was abandoned in 1824, when the little remnant of the Indian congregation went to Canada to join the mission there.

Yea, face to face I would behold
My David,[14] patriarch of the fold.

The helpers in his triumphs too,
And sharers of his toil, I'd view;
Besides, our Brother Schnall[15] I'd try
To see, and my heart satisfy.

Good Brother Heckewelder rode
With us along the Goshen road,
Through the late-purchased Brethren's-land,
All which he made me understand.

My God, what feelings then were raised,
When first upon the place I gazed

---

[14] David Zeisberger, the "Apostle of the Indians," born April 11, 1721, at Zauchtenthal, in Moravia, lived, a venerable sire of 82 years, in the midst of his "brown flock," to whom his life had been devoted, in his own house at Goshen. There too he died, after 62 years of unremitting labor for the salvation of the Indians, on Nov. 17, 1808; and there his humble grave is still pointed out to the visitor, under the shade of a kindly tree, on the old Goshen graveyard. A mere sketch even of his life would needs fill a volume.

[15] Missionary at Fairfield; attended the Conference as deputy from that place; retired to Bethlehem after the destruction of the mission at Fairfield by Gen. Harrison's troops, after the battle of the Thames, Oct. 5, 1813.

Which I had yearned so long to see,
And oft indeed not hopefully !

And, oh, what joy in me up-welled
When David's self I now beheld,
Surrounded as in Heaven 'twill be,
By brown and white souls equally.

And when I gave him my first kiss,
And he his greeting sealed with his,
How were my heart's affections moved,
And oh, how deeply I him loved !

Nor tongue nor pen can e'er express
How great was our happiness,
As heart with heart in love we blend,
He *Jonathan's,* I *David's* friend !

With warmest love we also greet
The lively Susel,[16] whom we meet,
And who as David's helpmate here
Surrounds him with good Christian cheer.

[16] On his last visit to the settlements in the East, Zeisberger, who had never been married, yielded to the advice of his friends, and though 60 years of age, was married at Lititz, in the spring of 1781, to Miss Susan Lecron. She was 23 years his junior, having been born at Lancaster on Feb. 17, 1744. She died at Bethlehem on Sept. 8, 1824, aged 80 years.

And Brother *Mortimer* and wife,
Who both here dedicate their life
To serve the Indians' highest weal,
With love and joy and fervent zeal.

And Brother *Haven*,[17] who essays
To serve the Lord in David's ways,
And does it most successfully—
We greet them all most fervently.

And little *Benjy Mortimer*[18]
Was not forgot : for sure we are
That him the Lord will too ordain,
And send him heathen souls to gain.

Soon the *brown flock* did also come,
And greet us, after their custom ;

[17] John Ben Haven had come to assist in the mission work at Goshen from Fulneck, in England, late in autumn of 1802 ; was ordained by Bishop Loskiel on the last day of the Conference ; and in spring of 1804 led a colony from Fairfield to the Pettquotting.

[18] Br. Mortimer's son's name was not Benjamin, but Joseph Warner Mortimer, this being the name given him in baptism by Bishop Loskiel, on October 29th, just before his departure for Bethlehem.

Bill Henry,[19] a most reverend man,
Led like a patriarch the van.

We kissing *them*—they kissing *us :*
O 'twas a sight most glorious,
And ne'er can be forgotten here,
Nor 'fore the *heathen's Saviour* There !

They who had brought us to this place,
Now straightway must their steps retrace,
To Gnadenhutten, where they are,
Besides their horses, lodged with care.

Us two a little house they gave,
Which for us they prepared have,

---

[19] One of the most notable converts ever made from among
the Indians of North America. His Indian name was Gciele-
mend ; he was born in 1737, near the Lehigh Gap, in Northampton Co., Pa.; rose to be one of the most eloquent orators, wise
counsellers, and brave and powerful chiefs the Delaware nation
ever had. He was converted in 1788, and in baptism took the
name of William Henry, after Judge Henry, the Congressman,
who once had done him a great favor. By a special covenant
the oldest son of this chief's descendants in each generation was
to take this same name. A great-grandson of his, the Rev. John
Killbuck, is at present (1887) a Moravian missionary among the
Eskimo in Western Alaska. Gelelemend died at Goshen in 1811—
died as he had lived, a devout and consistent Christian, a great
and noble man.

And which so homelike did appear,
I could live in it many a year.

Rose Anna next was domiciled
With David—she just like a child
With everything so pleased has been ;
Would Bethlehem could her have seen !

As you who know her heart's good bent
Can think, she found her element
There 'mong those brown ones, whom she loved,
So that her joy could not be moved.

But while such gladness filled us all,
None knew a word of Brother *Schnall*.
'Midst many doubts, and secret fear,
I scarce had hope to meet him here.

But suddenly, that self-same day—
A true Thanksgiving Day I say,—
"Schnall has arrived!" so some one cried,
And "Hallelujah!" echoed wide.

How gracious are the Saviour's ways!
Such kindness did us all amaze.
It was the work of Him alone!
What I had wished, lo, it was done!

Upon the neck I joyous fall,
Of this my dearest Brother Schnall!
Who out of a great sorrow came,
And comfort found in Jesus' name.

Thus all who'd been expected are
Assembled both from near and far,
And Conference hold in sweet accord,
Our work commending to the Lord.

Here then I close my humble rhyme;
But as Rose Anna has the time,
She's not forbidden yet to say
What more transpired from day to day.

CONCLUSION OF THE JOURNEY.

Now thank we all our God,
In Goshen's Friedenshutten,[20]
On Woapamikunk,[21]
In Fairfield,[22] Gnadenhutten,
And on Jonquanamik![23]
The Lord has so much done;
O worship Him with me,
Low bending 'fore His throne.
He gave us strength and grace,
To bring to right fruition
What we resolved had,
And in our plan's completion
His perfect will t' obey,
That so we truly might
The highest weal subserve
Of all, both brown and white.
No more from me. The rest
Must be by Rose related,
For she the talent hath

---

[20] So called here with indirect reference to the settlement of Moravian Indians at Bethlehem named thus, and with direct reference to the meaning of the name: "Tents of Peace."

[21] A Delaware Indian village on the White River, Indiana, near which the Moravians started a mission in spring 1801, with fifteen converts.

[22] A Moravian Indian village on the Thames river, Oxford Township, Canada, whence Goshen had been settled; destroyed in 1813.

[23] A temporary mission, on the stream of the same name, commenced by the Moravians from Fairfield among the Chippewas in 1802 or 1803.

In detail to narrate it,
Nor leave a thing untold.
To her I also leave
To tell of our return ;
Therefor she'll thanks receive.
But Thou, most gracious Lord,
Of all the mighty Ruler,
Accept my offered praise,—
Unworthy though the offerer—
For all Thy faithful love
Wherewith Thou us hast led,
And kept us whole and well,
With nothing we need dread.
Now, at our journey's end,
Let yet Thy blood most precious
Suffuse our sinful hearts,
In Thine own way most gracious !
Seal unto each of us,
To all eternity,
What Thou to our hearts
Hast given lovingly !
O, holy Three in One,
Speak Thy divine Amen
Unto our pilgrimage,
In Thy name underta'en !
Thy blessing rest thereon,
And on all that was done
At our Conference.
Complete what was begun !
Then honor, thanks, and praise,
To Thee, O Lord, be sung,

Already here on earth,
By *white* and *brown* men's tongue !
Till our course we end,
And Thee behold, Jehovah !
And all above, below,
Shout Amen, Hallelujah !

THE END.

www.ingramcontent.com/pod-product-compliance
Lightning Source LLC
Chambersburg PA
CBHW030709110426
42739CB00031B/1442